Published by
Vegan Publishers
Danvers, MA
www.VeganPublishers.com
©2018 Amber Pollock
Cover art and designs by Kayleigh Castle
Illustrations by Kayleigh Castle

ISBN: 978-1-940184-47-0

To my kids-
For making me see
the world differently.

What Vegan Kids Eat!

By **Amber Pollock**

Illustrated by **Kayleigh Castle**

VP Vegan Publishers™

Growing vegan awareness one book at a time.

f /veganpublishers   VeganPublishers.com

I am vegan and I slurp smoothies every morning
Starting each day this way is remarkably rewarding
Blended up with bananas and cherries
Don't forget the spinach and berries!

I am **vegan** and I go to school
Eating animals is **never** cool
Mom packed my favorite picks
Broccoli,
apples,
and carrot sticks

I am vegan and I eat after-school snacks
I cover everything with chia, hemp, and flax
Tangy chickpea hummus is my go-to treat
But when we are out,

      I find other snacks to eat

I am vegan
and fall is my favorite season
I can give you more than
one million reasons
I pick crunchy apples and
drink warm cider
And toast marshmallows
over an open fire

For dinner we have garlicky soup
While we sit by the fire and recoup

Afterward,
we drink some bedtime tea
While Mom and Dad read stories to me

I am vegan and I eat autumn's bounty
At the table with Mom, Dad, and my favorite auntie

Creamy mashed potatoes,
    green bean casserole,

        Zesty cranberry sauce,
            and buttery rolls

Candied yams and pumpkin pie
Our holiday feast is piled sky high

See, there's no room for turkey on this table

Now would you please
pass the gravy, Aunt Mable?

I am vegan
and the winter season grows colder

Comfort foods pop with flavor
and become bolder

The best is Mom's vegetable pot pie
with flaky crust

On a cold winter night,
it is an absolute must

We are snowed in, so Dad is making lunch
His ooey-gooey cashew cheeze packs a punch
Melt it between toasted bread
for his famous grilled cheeze
Dip it in tomato soup,
and I'll take more,
please

I am vegan and it's Christmas Eve night

Will Santa come?

I'm hoping he might!

I leave the almond milk and cookies by the tree
Hoping he will bring some wonderful
gifts for me

I am vegan and
Christmas morning has come

Last night
I dreamed of dancing sugar plums
And what did I see when I opened my eyes?
Santa filled my stocking
with candy—surprise!

I am vegan
and it's New Year's Eve tonight
I enjoy sparkling juice
while we grab a bite
Pretzels, popcorn,
and mini pizzas too
The countdown begins
and the year
becomes
new!

I am vegan
and I have love and hearts on the mind
Mom and Dad leave a card
asking to be my valentine
Along with truffles and
chocolates that are so divine
Best part is,
all of it is mine!

I am vegan and I am sick
Boy oh boy, I feel ick!
Mom brings me
no-chicken noodle soup in bed
Dad reads me a story
and says to rest my head

I am vegan
  and spring is **finally here!**
From my Easter basket
  the candies begin to disappear...
How I love bunny chocolates,
      gummies, and lollipops
There is so much to eat—
      how will I stop?

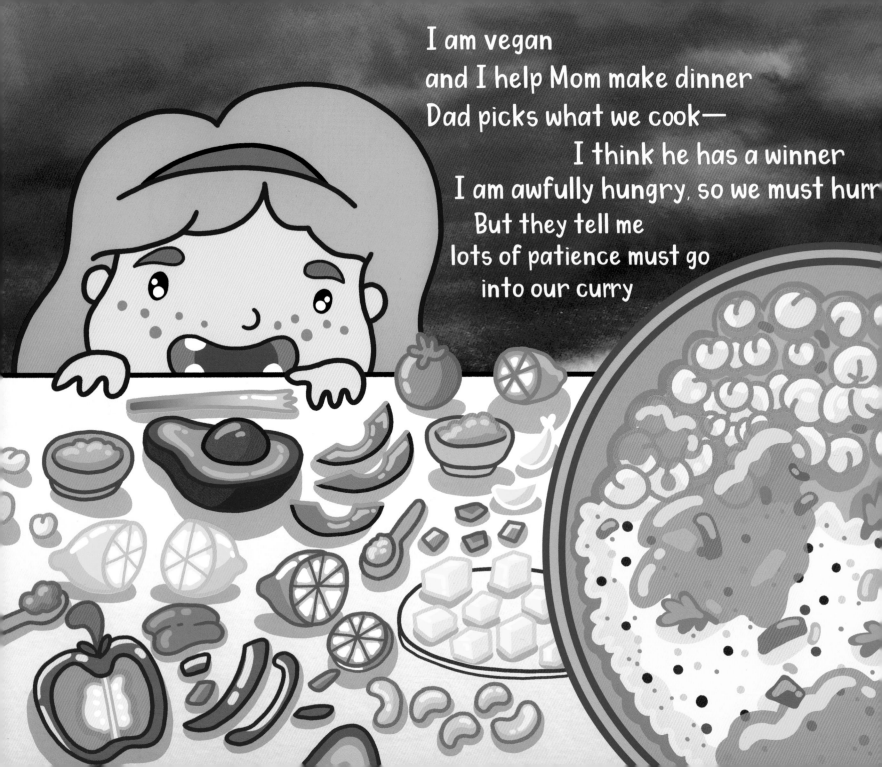

I am vegan
and I help Mom make dinner
Dad picks what we cook—
　　　　I think he has a winner
I am awfully hungry, so we must hurr
But they tell me
lots of patience must go
　　into our curry

I am vegan
   and today we picked from
   our vegetable patch
   (We even watched a nest of baby birds hatch)
We made huge salads
   after washing our fresh greens
      Piling plates with arugula,
         spinach, and
            crisp snap peas!

I am vegan
and I eat barbecue
on the Fourth of July
It is one of my
favorite days
'cause all my family comes by
My cousins think our
skewered veggies are lots of fun
But my favorite is
bean burgers
on Grandma's
homemade
buns!

I am vegan and it is storming,
    so we get out the Crock-Pot
I tell Mom,
"I think some chili would really hit the spot.
    Zucchini, corn, and tomatoes
        fresh from the ground
Then I add kidney, pinto,
        and black beans by the pound

I am vegan
and Mom and Dad bring me
breakfast in bed
Pancakes, an omelet, and
buttery potato shreds

I put on my new dress,
knowing this will
be the best day...
After all,

it is my birthday!

After breakfast
I help Mom bake
My favorite kind
of birthday cake
We hang a banner on our front gate
And soon my friends arrive
to help celebrate!

When I blow out the candles
on my birthday cake
I make a wish for
the animals' sake
I wish all my friends
would go vegan with me
And live their lives cruelty-free!

I am vegan

and I eat lots of things, you see
And vegan food tastes
the best to me
It's not just about
being in the mood

Animals are not harmed
for any of my food

Come sit down and
have a meal with me

And I think
you will soon agree...

Vegan
is the way to be!